LOOKING AT INLAND WATERWAYS

JOHN GAG

GW00802318

BROAᴅ

CANALS

First published 1977
© John Gagg 1977
ISBN 0 9504226 5 7

Published by John Gagg, Shootacre House, Princes Risborough, Buckinghamshire
Printed by Manson Graphic, 12 Frogmore Road, Apsley, Hemel Hempstead, Herts.

What is "Broad"?

Labelling canals "broad" or "narrow" isn't as easy as it sounds, since some canals don't fit exactly into either group. To make things more confusing, some canals are partly broad and partly narrow.

To start with, it's the width of the *locks*, and not of the canals themselves, that normally decides the label. Roughly, what we call narrow canals are those with locks less than 14ft wide — mostly 7ft, in fact. Broad canals are those with 14ft locks or wider. There are, however, some broad locks at the ends of the "narrow" Trent & Mersey, Shropshire Union, and Chesterfield Canals, and conversely, narrow locks on the Aylesbury, Northampton and Welford branches of the "broad" Grand Union, as well as at its Birmingham end.

The oddest fact is that the Leicester Main Line of the Grand Union has broad locks for 55 of its miles, but two bottlenecks of 17 narrow locks in its first 23 miles. I have included it as a broad canal, but because of the bottleneck much of it is officially classed as narrow. The Grand Union's Main Line to Birmingham, too, is surprisingly classed as narrow for most of its way, despite the locks being broad. This is mostly because of long tunnels where wide boats couldn't pass, and because of some narrow bridges. But with its 170 broad locks (including London sections), I have dealt with it as a broad canal.

One other point about labelling: there are quite a few waterways which have broad locks, but which are not in this book. These are the navigations which are almost entirely rivers such as the Trent or the Severn, or based on rivers, such as the Aire & Calder (though some of the latter have long canal stretches). The Soar Navigation might have been put with these, but since it is part of the Grand Union Leicester Line I have kept it with the "canals". The river-based navigations are gathered in a separate book.

This all sounds a bit confusing, but what it boils down to is that the canals in this book have most of their locks 14ft wide or more. Canals with narrower locks — usually 7ft — are described in the *Book of Narrow Canals*. Navigations mostly based on rivers are in the *Book of Cruising Rivers*.

Where canals have 14ft locks, then, 14ft-wide barges can use them, as they did in large numbers in the heyday of waterway commerce. Conveniently, too, a pair of 7ft-wide narrow boats from the narrow canals can go into such locks roped together side by side, as on the cover of this book. This is called "breasting up".

The Grand Union is the champion for sheer number of locks. The whole system with its branches has 212 broad locks as well as 63 narrow ones. In contrast the Ripon Canal now has only 1¼ miles and one lock left — the northernmost working canal lock in the waterway network in England. The Rochdale has about the same length remaining, in the middle of Manchester. But it still has nine locks left from the 92 which used to take it 33 miles over to Yorkshire.

These broad canals range from the Roman-built Fossdyke to the modern Manchester Ship Canal, and there are still two in Scotland. So they have much more variety in size and use than our narrow canals have — but not always the same peace and intimacy.

As with the *Book of Narrow Canals*, I have explored almost all these waterways by boat, and not merely read about them. I'm sorry if my boat intrudes too often into the photographs.

2

Bridgewater Canal

This canal, of course, is historically famous, though many think it dull to cruise along. It is always quoted as the forerunner of our canals, but this is hard on the Romans, the Exeter Canal, and the canalised Sankey Brook. All the same, the third Duke of Bridgewater certainly started something when he proposed to take coal by water to Manchester from his mines at Worsley.

John Gilbert designed the waterway, and had assisting him a man who became one of the famous names in waterway history — James Brindley. They worked from Worsley Old Hall, which still stands near the canal.

After the digging had started, a remarkable decision was taken. They agreed to cross the R. Irwell and run into Manchester to the south of the river. Taking a waterway across another on a bridge was an unbelievable idea, and it came in for much ridicule. But it worked, and the stone aqueduct remained until the much later building of the Manchester Ship Canal replaced it with an even more remarkable swinging one.

The original canal linked up with nearly 50 miles of underground mine waterways, from which the coal came out in distinctive boats nicknamed "starvationers". Later a longer canal section was dug towards Runcorn, to link with the Mersey. There is no link at Runcorn now, but there is one with the Trent & Mersey Canal. The original canal now also goes north from Worsley to join with the Leeds & Liverpool. The Bridgewater is owned by the Manchester Ship Canal, and not by British Waterways.

The northern arm brings boats south from the desolate areas near Leigh, and past parkland and nostalgic Worsley to the present Barton aqueduct. This swings full of water (800 tons of it) to allow ships to pass on the canal below. Then the route joins the canal from Manchester, and heads for Runcorn.

There are long built-up areas, with a railway alongside, before greener banks offer views northwards. Lymm is a pleasant halt before passing under the M6 and to the Warrington outskirts. Then again more open country, and from the many boats at Preston Brook a short run through rhododendrons to Runcorn. This developing town is linked with Widnes by a striking bridge over the Ship Canal and the Mersey.

39½ miles, 1 lock, 1 swing and 3 other big aqueducts. Opened 1761 to 1799.

Caledonian Canal

This is a very unusual and spectacular waterway compared with the others in this book. It has no link with any other, and in fact less than half of its 60 miles is "canal" — 38½ miles consist of Loch Lochy, Loch Oich, Loch Ness and Loch Dochfour. In the two bigger ones of Lochy and Ness the weather and waves can be just like the sea. The canal, of course, cuts Scotland in two from south-west to north-east.

The Lochs were linked by Telford to save sailing ships from the dangers and delays of rounding the north of Scotland. But soon many ships were too big for the canal locks, and steam-engines made the sea trip rather safer. To this day, though, fishing vessels and yachts make frequent use of the short cut, and there is an increase of straightforward pleasure cruising for its own sake, especially from the Inverness end.

The canal starts on the outskirts of Inverness at Clachnaharry, and soon climbs up four staircase locks to where British Waterways' *Scot II* starts her trips. Already the mountains are ahead, and only four miles of canal bring the first small loch, Dochfour, and then the 23 mighty miles of Loch Ness.

This is staggering country, monster or not, but canallers from England will find both cruising and mooring much more complicated. Loch Ness's water can be over 700ft deep, for example, and the sloping rocky shores must be avoided. The mountains soar up, however, either savage and sheep-covered, or planted with ranks of conifers. Lighthouses mark the canal exits and the south-western one is at Fort Augustus. A swing bridge and five staircase locks take boats higher still to a three-mile canal, with two more locks to the highest level of all in Loch Oich, 106ft above the sea.

Loch Oich is possibly the finest stretch of all for scenery, though boats must keep to the marked channel. Invergarry Castle leads them on to the massive Laggan cutting, and then down to Loch Lochy. This again is deep, with mountains covered in timber for the paper mill at Corpach. At its end, a six-mile canal leads to the striking eight-lock Banavie staircase — often forgotten when people look for the greatest staircase of locks in Britain. As in all staircases, craft pass from each lock straight to the next, with massive tall gates between. Then it is a short distance to the western sea-lock of the canal.

60 miles, 29 locks, 4 lochs, 11 swing bridges. Completed 1822.

Crinan Canal

The Crinan, the other Scottish canal still in full use, is on a much smaller scale than the Caledonian, though it too is a "short cut" canal. It saves the 132-mile journey round the long arm of the Mull of Kintyre, and thus boats from the Firth of Clyde can take this way to the Islands.

It was a difficult canal to dig through rock and peat, but when all its problems had been solved it emerged as a fine route, running along below the hills and above a wide, low stretch of mossland.

The western end, at Crinan village, is like a picture postcard, especially if you climb a hill and look down on it. There's a little lighthouse at the sea lock, a hotel looking out to the islands, and a collection of boats ranging from small cruisers through slick chromium yachts to tough fishing vessels. They come in here — often from rough weather — to make the nine-mile passage to Ardrishaig, or perhaps merely to shelter. Great balance beams on the lock-gates here used to move inch by inch only, however hard you pushed. Now the gates are mechanised.

Setting out eastwards, the canal runs just above the edge of Loch Crinan to a wide lagoon at Bellanoch. Much of this length is a narrow rocky trough, where bigger boats cannot pass each other. The route then starts inland, and the views north grow after five locks at Dunardry take it to its highest level.

Ardrishaig.

It soon drops down through four locks by a smart hotel at Cairnbaan, and runs along a valley towards Loch Gilp, which it reaches near the clean little town of Lochgilphead. It doesn't join the loch immediately, however, but runs alongside above the lochside road for two miles, dropping at last to Ardrishaig and the eastern sea lock. Again there are fishing boats and a little lighthouse, then the breadth of Loch Fyne and the route to the Clyde.

9 miles, 15 locks, 7 swing bridges. Completed 1809.

Erewash Canal

Mooring at Sandiacre, with the Red Lion *and the* White Lion *near.*

No-one would recommend the Erewash for spectacular scenery (though Stanton Ironworks at full blast was once spectacular enough), nor for drifting peacefully among the birds and the flowers. But it's an intriguing canal, all the same, in a one-time web of canals. It actually became in 1932 part of the Grand Union network, but it is usually named and described separately nowadays.

To bring coal from Nottinghamshire and Derbyshire collieries to the Soar and Loughborough, and then elsewhere by road at first, a canal was proposed from Langley Mill down the Erewash valley. It was then to cut across to the Trent almost opposite the Soar's mouth. No time was lost after the Act of Parliament, and the canal opened in 1779, 11¾ miles long with 14 locks, rising 109ft.

The Erewash sparked off much other activity. An extension northwards, the Cromford Canal, opened in 1794. This was a complicated task, with several aqueducts and the great Butterley tunnel, nearly 3,000yd long. The tunnel and the locks above were narrow, and by 1841 the Cromford and High Peak Railway (instead of a previously proposed canal link) joined the Cromford with the canals of the north-west.

The 4½-mile, 13-lock Nutbrook Canal brought coal and iron to the Erewash by about 1795, and by 1796 the Nottingham Canal brought competition by taking trade from the junction of the Cromford and the Erewash, direct to the city and the Trent. In 1796 also, the Derby Canal, from the Trent via Swarkestone and Derby, joined the Erewash at Sandiacre. Its Swarkestone-Trent length didn't last long.

So the Erewash was soon at the hub of quite a group of canals considering its short length, and was in fact one of the most prosperous canals in the country. But as usual, railways began to undermine that prosperity. They bought up surrounding canals and neglected them, though they never obtained the Erewash. At last it came under the Grand Union, but commerce had ceased by 1952.

Above Ilkeston it was officially unnavigable in 1962, but enthusiasts persisted, and now it is again used throughout. Indeed, the first lock of the Cromford Canal was restored in 1973, making 15 locks to navigate, and the basin at the junction of the Erewash, Cromford and Nottingham Canals was brought back into valuable use again.

The canal's entrance lock is at an awkward spot where the boater from the Soar may be confused. A dangerous weir takes the Trent to his right, and next comes the navigation cut for the river towards Nottingham. The Erewash is across the Trent at an angle to the left.

There are two pubs here, one having changed its name for some reason from the *Fisherman's Rest* to the *Steamboat*, the other having the good old *Navigation* name. Then past a boatyard and houseboats, and a collection of railways, the canal comes to Long Eaton. Factories are offset by some pleasant back gardens, before a mass of railway sidings across the R. Erewash.

At Sandiacre the Derby Canal remains can be seen above the lock, and there is a pleasant shopping halt by a busy crossroads. A rather more rural stretch comes before the M1 crosses, then the once-roaring Stanton Ironworks dominates the canal. The Nutbrook used to come in here, but is now just a couple of pipes.

Stensons lock and Awsworth rail viaduct

There are playing fields to the right, then the main road to Ilkeston, but the R. Erewash and now the remains of the Nottingham canal keep the right-hand view uncluttered still. There is a great trestle rail viaduct in the distance, and at Shipley lock the site of former tram and rail lines down from collieries to the canal. There is also a superior pub off to the left, and old stables on the right at the lock.

Over the river now to Eastwood lock, and on a rural length at last to Langley Mill. Past a factory and a busy road is the revived lock into the Great Northern Basin.

11¾ miles, 15 locks now, 1 aqueduct. Completed 1779.

Exeter Ship Canal

Short and sharp, and rarely visited even by canal enthusiasts, the Exeter is at least famous historically as Britain's first canal with locks. The original canal, engineered by John Trew in 1566, has been lengthened and changed a good deal, and of course the locks are quite different now from the first ones, which perhaps had vertical gates. The first canal was only 16ft wide and 3ft deep, but later its upper width was made 94ft, with 15ft of depth.

There is only one lock along the canal's route, but there is a side-lock to the Exe opposite Topsham, which was the port of Exeter at one time. The canal once started at this lock, but the present entrance lock, Turf lock, is now further down the estuary. Near Exeter itself some flood-gates connect with the river when the tide is level. Coasters up to 400 tons can use the canal.

There is a short approach channel from the Exe, then Turf lock raises the canal to run alongside the estuary facing Topsham, a pleasant place with boats in the river. Then the waterway continues a lonely run to the notorious Exeter road by-pass at Countess Wear, with its swing bridge. The original weir here blocked the Exe and led to the digging of the canal.

Gates at Double Locks.

Rural swing bridge.

A little further is Double Locks — only one lock in fact — 25ft wide with huge balance beams, and a pub of the same name alongside. This is a sort of no-man's-land, despite the nearness of road, rail and city.

And so the canal comes to the basin short of the main river bridge at Exeter. This basin has been kept in good last-century shape, with stone buildings housing the Exeter Maritime Museum between the canal and the river, and many historical craft ashore and afloat, from Welsh coracles to Bude Canal tub-boats.

5 miles, 3 locks, 4 swing bridges. Built 1566-1830.

Fossdyke Canal

The shades of the Romans must laugh at all the history books which talk of the Bridgewater as our "first canal". For they dug the Fossdyke more than 1,600 years earlier, and it's still working.

It joins the Trent at Torksey with the Witham at Lincoln, and was used over the years by both invaders and inhabitants, including the carrying of stone to build Lincoln Cathedral. But use fell away, and both the canal and the Witham were almost unnavigable at one time.

The city of Lincoln became responsible for the Fossdyke, and made improvements in the 18th century. Both canal and river were straightened at different times, and Grand Sluice at Boston was built to keep out the tides. Much of the work was also concerned with draining the low-lying countryside.

Even this ancient waterway at last came under railway control. There was still some trade to Lincoln up to a few years ago, but little is likely now. Pleasure boats must pass a tidal Trent length to reach the canal, so it remains a quiet waterway.

Unusual lock gear at the entrance from the Trent.

The lock at Torksey has a keeper, and it has extra gates to keep the Trent out if necessary. Many boats moor in the safety of the canal, but after passing them there is deserted country, with high banks at times hiding the flat views. There are straight runs, too, but at a bend a main road joins the canal for a time, and there are shops, pubs and fish and chips alongside at Saxilby.

Again houses disappear, though now a railway is near. An isolated building on the left turns out to be a pub called the *Pyewipe* — old word for peewit — and beyond it Lincoln Cathedral is distant on its hill. Then, near the racecourse, the city begins. There is a lift-bridge, and suddenly Brayford Pool. This is a wide sheet of water, now hopefully being made pleasant in the heart of Lincoln.

The Witham comes in at one corner, and leaves at another to run under the famous "Glory Hole" bridge, with its half-timbered building. Boats can moor in Brayford, while their crews climb the steep hill to the cathedral.

11 miles, 1 lock, 1 lift-bridge. First dug about AD120.

Gloucester & Sharpness Ship Canal

On a smaller scale than the Manchester Ship Canal, this one is nevertheless much bigger than the usual "broad" canals of this book. It has no locks except at its ends, but the size of vessel using it is intriguingly shown by the width of its one lift-bridge and 15 swing bridges. It's an alarming sight to see a towering ship squeezing through one of them, and scars on their side-posts proclaim strong winds or slight steering errors. An unusual feature is the architecture of the portico-ed bridge-keepers' houses at many of the bridges.

The Severn has long been a water highway, with boats trading even up to Welshpool at one time. Gangs of men hauled them, especially on the upper reaches, though later a towing-path was built for horses. Tolls were once paid for nearly 400 horses for this work. The river was always difficult with currents and shallows, but there were special problems in the length below Gloucester.

This was dangerous, shifting, and strongly tidal. Vessels would ground, or be caught by the famous Severn bore. So the idea of an artificial cut was discussed, including the possibility of a canal from Gloucester to Bristol. Eventually a ship canal was approved in 1793 from Gloucester to Berkeley Pill lower down the Severn. It was intended, of course, for bigger vessels than those on the river above Gloucester.

Construction was a different task from ordinary canal digging, and proved expensive. After a few years it looked as if it might even be abandoned, although Gloucester docks were being built, and over five miles of so-far-useless canal had been dug. The government had to step in, and on Telford's recommendation work began again, with the aid of government money and to a slightly different terminus at Sharpness. It took till 1827 to finish the task, but to give credit, it was the largest-dimension canal in the world at that time.

Since then commerce has faded away on the Severn but the canal, luckily, continues in its own right. Traffic runs to Gloucester, or to places below it, and ironically Sharpness docks themselves form one of the most profitable assets of the British Waterways Board.

There is of course no great variety of scenery in the 16 miles. A lock leads up from the Severn into Gloucester docks, where some magnificent old warehouses and even a sailors' church exist in a surprising inland port. Then a new lifting bridge leads out to the canal.

Gloucester Docks.

The first length is industrial, alongside a busy road and including stacks of timber. Then a Z-bend takes you into more rural surroundings. There are traffic-lights at the swing bridges, and just before Sellars Bridge a row of oil-tanks fed from oil-tankers. The Severn, though not far away, is invisible, and there is hardly a building to be seen at times.

Saul is interesting, for there the Stroudwater Canal comes up from the river and crosses on the level. There are many boats moored on it for a short distance, but the rest is at present derelict, though with a vigorous restoration Trust at work. There is rather more sign of civilisation here, past Frampton, but again empty countryside for a while.

From Patch Bridge, with two pubs, you can visit the famous Slimbridge Wildfowl Trust, on the land between canal and river. Then a long lonely run, without even a bridge, takes the canal to a huge new waterworks at Purton, with again two pleasant pubs as well as two close bridges worked by the same keeper.

The river is visible below now, wide and wild-looking. There are old timber ponds by the canal where timber used to be kept afloat, and the remains of the once-tall rail bridge over canal and river — damaged by a vessel on the river in 1959, and now almost entirely removed. Then to the right is the old disused Sharpness basin, the arm to it full of pleasure boats. Ahead are the busy docks, leading to the vast sea-lock out to the estuary.

There is, of course, a rapid rise and fall of the tide outside, and the lock only operates for a short time around high water. The river is no place for inland pleasure boats, but steerers with tidal experience and well-equipped boats make the trip to the Avon, Bristol and Bath.

16 miles, 2 locks, 16 movable bridges. Completed 1827.

11

Grand Union Canal (London to Birmingham)

Braunston spire — famous Grand Union landmark.

This is the most complicated canal of the lot, especially historically. It's also quite tricky trying to follow it on the map in places. We look at the line through Leicester separately on pages 15—16, and the Erewash Canal on pages 6—7, so let's try here to sort out the London to Birmingham route.

The present name for the system dates in fact only from 1929, though "Grand Union" was earlier used for what is now part of the Leicester line (now often called the "Old Grand Union"). An amalgamation in 1929, extended later, brought the following canals under the revived name:

Hertford Union Canal, R. Lee to Regent's Canal;

Regent's Canal, R. Thames to Grand Junction Paddington Branch;

Grand Junction Canal, Paddington Branch and Brentford to Braunston;

Warwick and Napton Canal (five miles of the Oxford Canal link Braunston and Napton);

Warwick and Birmingham Canal;

Birmingham and Warwick Junction Canal (link to the Birmingham & Fazeley).

(see pages 15—16 for the *Old Grand Union*, the *Leicestershire and Northamptonshire Union,* the *Leicester Navigation* and the *Loughborough Navigation*, and pages 6—7 for the *Erewash Canal*)

The Grand Union system thus had two links with the Thames — Brentford and Limehouse — and one with the Lee, the main lines then leading both to Birmingham and the Trent. The Birmingham line has branches from Slough, Aylesbury and Northampton, and at one time there were many smaller branches too. Besides the links with the Thames, Lee and Trent, there are connections with the R. Nene, the Oxford Canal, the Stratford Canal, the Birmingham & Fazeley Canal, and of course the Birmingham Canal Navigations with their many links north, west and south. Altogether the Grand Union is undoubtedly the king of our canal systems, and at one time was extremely busy, with its own large fleet of boats.

The history of all this is fascinating, and Charles Hadfield's books cover it in detail. Looking at the route nowadays, the locks to Birmingham are all broad except for the last 12 in Birmingham itself, but tunnels and some bridges make the use of 14ft boats rare. The Aylesbury and Northampton branches have 7ft locks (and plenty of them), and of course the locks in the connected Birmingham area are all narrow. So despite a lot of wishful widening expenditure in the 1930's, the whole of the GU system continued largely to use narrow boats. At least, however, they can go through the broad locks in pairs.

Today you may still find regular narrow boat trade near London and the occasional enthusiast elsewhere, usually selling coal. And many traditionally-painted narrow boats, converted or not to pleasure cruising, still scatter on this wide-flung group of canals.

In London, the eastern connection with the Thames is at Limehouse Basin, formerly called Regent's Canal Dock. This can only be entered from the river at certain states of the tide, then the canal runs up through the East End and several locks. The Hertford Union comes in from the Lee after 1¾ miles, and the route eventually reaches the Zoo after passing Victoria Park, the *Narrow Boat* pub by City Road Basin, Islington tunnel, St Pancras station, and the interesting canal area at Hampstead Road. It runs right through the Zoo by Lord Snowdon's birdcage and comes to famous Little Venice, crowded with boats and people in summer. Paddington Basin is up a short arm.

This is the Paddington branch now, running past Westway's stilts, gasworks, prison and cemetery, over the North Circular and by many factories to Bulls Bridge junction. This is where the other Thames link comes up from Brentford, with maybe trading boats climbing the Hanwell locks, like the pair below.

There are still Southall, West Drayton and Uxbridge to brave, and the intriguing five-mile Slough arm, with water lilies and surprising isolation, comes in on the way. Then at last you burst into the countryside at Denham.

It's real countryside, too, though houses are sometimes near. There are many lake-like gravel-pits nearby, and a wealth of flowers and birds. But the canal swings back towards Rickmansworth and Watford, though only skirting the latter by very pleasant Cassiobury Park. It then heads up the Gade valley, rather noisily near Inter-City trains and the A41, and through the pubs of Berkhamsted towards the Chilterns.

Cowroast lock is at the top, and a dull cutting leads to the downward slope by the old Wendover arm. After seven locks comes the 16-lock, 6¼-mile Aylesbury branch, to the town centre. The main line, still with fine views, drops and gradually levels as it cuts through Milton Keynes new city, the boats at Cosgrove, and at last to Stoke Bruerne's fine museum and thatched pub.

Blisworth's mighty tunnel now, wet and 3,056yd long, and nearly 15 level miles to the next locks at Buckby. On the way the 17-lock arm from Northampton and the R. Nene enters, and still Inter-City trains roar by, and the M1 also at times. Whilton Marina is below the locks, and after the top lock the line to Leicester goes off (see pages 15—16). Another vast tunnel, 2,042yd, takes you to Braunston, then and now a thriving boat-centre and a historic canal village.

The GU now shares the Oxford Canal for five miles before turning off to the first new-type locks of the improvements of the thirties. Altogether there are 51 of these, with striking leaning enclosed paddle-gear, working on a worm principle. Beyond Royal Leamington Spa — rather notorious for neglecting its canal — 21 of these locks climb up closer and closer, the Golden Steps to Heaven. Warwick can be seen as you climb.

Warwickshire locks near Stockton.

Eight well-deserved level miles pass a short tunnel and the junction with the Stratford Canal — a short link where this canal runs close by. Then the five Knowle locks are the last of the broad type.

Past Solihull, surprisingly, there is much floating rubbish and some rather dreary stretches before Birmingham's factories grip you. Among the Camp Hill narrow locks is a place like the depths of Hades, then an intriguing junction with rope-marks deep in the metal bridge-rails. To the left is a link across to the Birmingham network, and to the right the great Grand Union runs its last grubby 2½ miles. It ends at the Birmingham & Fazeley Canal under the Spaghetti Junction tangle of motorways, which must cause the spirits of the canal builders many a sleepless night.

(All sections) 176¼ miles, 215 locks, 5 tunnels, 4 main and many smaller aqueducts. Parts opened from 1800.

14

Grand Union Canal (Leicester line)

This length of the Grand Union leaves the Birmingham line at Norton junction and runs up through Foxton, Leicester and Loughborough to the Trent. The Erewash Canal across the Trent is also strictly part of the GU system, but I dealt with it on pages 6–7.

The line to the Trent was originally four different navigation companies:

(Old) Grand Union Canal, Norton to Foxton;

Leicestershire & Northamptonshire Union Canal, Market Harborough—Foxton—Leicester;

Leicester Navigation, Leicester to Loughborough;

Loughborough Navigation, Loughborough to the Trent.

The coming together of these makes a story rather more interesting than most.

The last two waterways are river navigations based on the Soar, with the Trent to Loughborough section working as early as 1778. As with so many waterways, the extension from Loughborough to Leicester was much concerned with competition between coalfields for trade. In fact a fascinating canal — the Charnwood Forest — was dug as part of the scheme, to bring coal to a tramroad which ran 2½ miles downhill to Loughborough and the water again. Unhappily this canal never worked very well, and after many difficulties was abandoned in 1848.

The Soar was navigable up to Leicester by 1794, and people then began to look southwards. There were various changes and complications, with money running out and over-elaborate plans, but eventually a canal to Market Harborough was dug by the Leicestershire & Northamptonshire Union, and the (Old) Grand Union Canal Co. dug one from the LNU at Foxton to the Grand Junction at Buckby. And since the Grand Junction came up from the Thames, what had happened — remarkably — was that Leicester was linked with London as well as with the Trent.

The only odd-looking thing was that the locks on the Old GU were made narrow, though all the locks both north and south were broad. Later this was regretted, and the fascinating Foxton Inclined Plane was built in 1900 to take broad boats up and down. It must have been a striking sight, but unhappily the other locks were never widened, and the plane went out of use in 1910.

So that, in a nutshell, is the story of the variegated Leicester line of the present Grand Union, and how a vital part of this broad route remains "narrow".

There are in fact only two groups of narrow locks, but they are 21 miles apart. The first seven are at Watford (Northants), close to the M1 shortly after the route leaves the Birmingham line. Four of them are in a staircase, and after the locks the lonely winding 21 miles soon bring you to Crick tunnel. There is no village on the journey, though some are near. There is a branch to Welford and another tunnel near Husbands Bosworth, and then with only sheep for company you reach the other locks at the Foxton end.

These are often spectator-ridden in summer, being in two staircases of five locks each with a short central passing place. There is confusion at busy times, for of course boats cannot pass in a narrow-boat staircase. At the bottom the 5½-mile branch to Market Harborough leaves, and the main line soon reaches its third tunnel at Saddington, ghost and all. Again villages are distant, and often the canal is shallow as scattered locks are passed. Then there is a long, slow entry to Leicester.

This is not a salubrious length, but the Soar section beyond becomes pleasant at Birstall. There is a restaurant by Cossington lock, then a busy boating area at Mountsorrel with a pub at the lockside. At Barrow the route leaves the river and goes past backyards to Loughborough. The basin is to the left, and to the right you rejoin the Soar after two locks.

Two views on the Soar near Mountsorrel.

The channel is wider now, past Normanton's squat church and many water-meadows. The *White House* overlooks you with a balcony, but Kegworth is difficult to reach across the weir stream. The last lonely stretch leads to the looming power station near Redhill lock. From here, precariously, you join the Trent, bearing left upriver to avoid a powerful weir. The Erewash Canal is opposite then, the Trent & Mersey further upriver, and the Cranfleet Cut to Nottingham and the Trent again is second on the right.

73¼ miles, 58 locks (+ 2 flood locks), 3 tunnels. Parts opened between 1778 and 1814.

16

Huddersfield Broad Canal (Sir John Ramsden's)

If you cruise this canal you won't forget it in a hurry. The locks are hard work, the views are striking, there's a remarkable lift-bridge, and you end the short but hard slog in a pleasant basin by a roaring road a stone's throw from the town.

Sir John Ramsden's family owned almost all Huddersfield in the 1770s, and thought a canal link with the Calder & Hebble Navigation would be a good thing. So with nine locks the canal stepped down to Cooper Bridge to make the junction. Later, the now-closed Huddersfield Narrow Canal continued the other way, 20 miles and 74 locks over the Pennines, with Britain's longest tunnel as a bottleneck on the journey.

The canal certainly brought coal, lime and prosperity to Huddersfield, carrying away its woollen goods. But now it carries only intrepid pleasure-boaters.

They turn sharply back left from the Calder & Hebble above Cooper Bridge flood gates, then sharp right away from the weir and into the first lock. There are plenty of trees and fields interspersed by factories at first, but little time to look as the locks are worked. Windlasses don't always fit, some gates are stiff to open, and the curious curved metal bollards are helpful for tying boats. Balance-beams are sometimes angled to suit the bridges.

Luckily the locks cease a mile from the end, so you can appreciate the industrial views backed by moors. Then comes the lift bridge, which is unchained by a special key, and wound up bodily by means of chains and pulleys. Avoid it in factory rush hours.

Round the corner beyond is the basin and Aspley Marina, with road traffic to keep you awake at night. The Narrow Canal is lost now under the road, but you can find it again beyond. And you can climb the hill to the town centre, which seems full mainly of coffee-shops now.

3¼ miles, 9 locks, 1 lift bridge. Completed 1776.

Kennet & Avon Canal

Restoration has brought boats to Hungerford again.

No two canals present the same picture, but the "K & A" is undoubtedly different from any other. Running from Thames to Severn, it is — or will be again — a great broad-beam route across England, the only one besides the Leeds & Liverpool, and indeed the only southern way of linking eastern and western waterways without the present detour through Birmingham. Its especial claim to fame is that it refused to die; and thanks to the Kennet & Avon Canal Trust it is vigorously on the way to restoration, despite formidable obstacles.

It is an odd navigation, in that it is two rivers joined by a canal. The Avon had long been used to Bristol, and in 1727 was made navigable to Bath, with six locks. At the other end of the country 18½ miles of the Kennet, with 21 locks, linked Newbury with the Thames at Reading by 1723. This idea of joining the two rivers had been abroad since the days of the first Elizabeth.

After some extraordinary manoeuvring, and several surveys, digging began in 1794, and a linking canal was opened in 1810 from Newbury to Bath. Gradually the Kennet, and the majority of the Avon company shares, came under the control of the one company.

The navigation was busy for a time, with barges between London and Bristol taking nine days, and some narrow boats even doing the trip in five. The Somersetshire Coal Canal — despite problems in dealing with steep slopes — had opened in 1805, and became a great supplier of trade to the K & A. At various times it was served by 31 pits.

Unhappily the K & A was one of those canals which suffered especially badly from railway competition when it came. The Great Western from London to Bristol, opened in 1841, made an immediate impact, and the railway eventually acquired the canal in 1852.

From then on was the usual story — a canal as the poor relation of its railway owners. Trade fell away and some canal lengths deteriorated, yet traffic doggedly persisted in places. There are stirring stories of through journeys even up to 1951. A huge petition was carried from Bristol to London by canoe in 1956, and the Kennet & Avon Canal Trust has kept restoration continually in the public eye.

At present the waterway is in several separated usable parts, with work busy extending each. The Reading length has a drab start from the Thames, but then becomes rural, and with a few turf-sided locks and some swing bridges heads for the first restoration area. Then there is an unnavigable stretch, at the moment, before the Newbury section.

This of course is where the canal proper begins, and Newbury is where much of the canal restoration fight has centred. The K & A CT uses one of the old wharf buildings, though the former basin now holds wheeled vehicles. This part is now a delightful cruising waterway with many boats on it. Past Hamstead Park and extensive woods it reaches Kintbury, with two superior eating-places by the lock. Still in the flat Kennet valley, it arrives at the interesting town of Hungerford. Already this restored part goes beyond, cocking a snook at the railway always close by. There is then a gap still to be filled.

In this gap is the famous Crofton pumping station, and the reservoir which sends water up to the summit level. This level is usable, with Bruce tunnel and four locks down to the 15-mile Long Pound past Pewsey. Then comes Devizes and the steep derelict lock-flight of 29 locks, a striking sight in aerial photographs, and a costly and challenging job.

Beyond the beauty spot of Bradford-on-Avon is a length of canal which was long the "dry section", through leaks and landslips. This may well, by the time this is being read, have been sealed and filled with water again. There are two fine aqueducts along the route to Bath — Avoncliffe and Dundas — and the water-driven Claverton pump.

In Sydney Gardens, Bath, with the old canal offices in the distance.

Now at last Bath, through pleasant Sydney Gardens and down six restored locks (formerly seven) to the Avon. This is different cruising now, and six more locks complete the official K & A to Hanham, with Bristol and the Severn beyond.

86½ miles, 104 locks now, 3 tunnels, 2 main aqueducts. Completed 1810.

Lancaster Canal

There are several sad things about the Lancaster. In the first place, it never became what it was intended to become, and ended up being cut off from other waterways for ever. To add a late insult to this, its most scenic northern part was chopped off and lost in 1955. And at the other end Preston seems to ignore its very existence now.

Reluctant present terminus at Tewitfield.

There's a curious thing about it, too. All the maps and guides now show it running north from Preston through Lancaster to the abrupt terminus at Tewitfield by the M6 motorway. But in fact there's 10¾ miles of it also happily existing between Wigan top lock and Johnson's Hillock locks, via Adlington and Chorley. This was in fact leased to the Leeds & Liverpool Canal long ago, and became part of it.

The Lancaster was intended to run from Westhoughton, a few miles east of Wigan, all the way to Kendal, crossing the wide rivers Ribble and Lune. In the end the "South End" was dug from Wigan to Walton Summit, about four miles short of the Ribble and Preston, and the "North End" from Preston to Kendal. Despite many plans, the two parts were eventually linked only by a horse tramroad across the river. In time the South End was cut off for good, to the L & L's benefit.

The origins of the canal were partly the usual superiority of water transport over the roads of the day, and partly the difficulty of sea-trade to Lancaster up the shifty Lune. A canal could link Lancaster with Preston and perhaps the rest of Lancashire, as well as with the districts northwards, carrying the usual coal, and such goods as grain, limestone and slate from the north.

Although the Ribble aqueduct was never built, there is a magnificent one over the Lune, upriver from Lancaster. Designed by Rennie, it is a striking sight in stone (though Rennie talked of brick). It is 600ft long and 60ft above the river, with five arches. Other aqueducts had to be built to cross the rivers Keer, Conder, Wyre and Brock.

The Lancaster had a complicated history of negotiation with the new railways, running some of its own at one time, but selling out in the end. It also took an exceptional interest in fast passenger boats, probably because it had only eight locks between Preston and Kendal. They kept going, with many changes of horses, at around 10 mph.

Nowadays the canal starts grubbily in Preston, but soon reaches pleasant country with wide views, apart from one splodge of industry. Trees often run alongside, and there are moored boats and a hire base at Catforth. At Duncombe the M6 appears, and at Garstang there is a basin with a restaurant and museum in a converted barn. Delightful mileposts appear regularly.

The Pennine foothills are eastwards, through more empty country, and at Lodge Hill the unusual sight of locks under a side-bridge indicates the branch down to Glasson. This runs for 2½ miles to Glasson Basin, with a small port on the Lune which was once part of the canal plan. The main line passes another big boatyard at Galgate before starting its run into Lancaster.

Gnarled steps — Hest Bank.

Tough paddle-gear on the Glasson branch.

The city now makes a little more fuss of its canal, which runs up the Lune before crossing the great aqueduct. It then heads back towards the sea, and passes within a stone's throw of it (but above it) at Hest Bank, where transhipment once took place. You can see the Lake District mountains across Morecambe Bay. There are pleasant houses at Bolton-le-Sands, then the canal slinks past behind Carnforth before going under the M6.

The Keer aqueduct is by an old quarry, and through quiet country you reach the tidy present terminus at Tewitfield. The derelict locks are beyond an embankment, and there is still water in much of the cut-off canal towards Kendal.

45 miles, 6 locks, 5 river aqueducts. Opened Preston-Tewitfield 1799.

Leeds & Liverpool Canal

The Grand Union may be the longest and most complicated canal system, but the Leeds & Liverpool is undoubtedly the grandest. Everything about it is on a grand scale — its miles of Pennine scenery, its stone-built locks and bridges, its 50-plus swing bridges, its remarkable variety of unusual paddle-gear, its collection of staircase locks, and its general air of solid immortality.

Moorland moorings.

Unusual lock-gear.

In fact it seems to deter some pleasure-boaters, who may feel that it is hard work. But there are some stretches which are gentle enough, though the 17 moorland miles without locks from Bingley to Gargrave are deceptive, for there are 25 bridges to be swung. On the map it seems to be over-supplied with industrial towns such as Leeds, Burnley, Blackburn and Wigan, but in fact it seems to get through most of them surprisingly easily, and even among their factories there are always sweeping valleys with moorland rising beyond.

The L & L is the only remaining trans-Pennine waterway, though there are revival moves for both the broad Rochdale and the Huddersfield Narrow. Crossing the backbone of England was a formidable task, and completion took more than 40 years, with the highest level reaching 487ft above the sea.

The first steps in this 127¼-mile canal really had no connection with crossing the Pennines. They were the development, during the 18th century, of the Douglas Navigation from Wigan to the Ribble, and this route is still bound up with the present canal. It was in 1766 that a Yorkshire meeting talked of linking Hull with Liverpool by joining the Aire at Leeds to the Mersey at Liverpool, with tremendous advantages to the many towns between east and west coasts.

A Yorkshire part from Bradford to Gargrave, and the route from Liverpool to the Douglas and Wigan were open by 1774, and the Yorkshire end reached Leeds and the Aire in 1777. But there was still quite a bit of argument over where to take the line in Lancashire, and in fact the Wigan to Colne length dithered for many years. At one stage the whole idea of an east-west link was in doubt, and the separate sections were quite busy in themselves.

After all the discussion, what eventually happened was that the L & L used over 10 miles of the "South End" of the already-dug Lancaster Canal, climbing up 23 locks to join it above Wigan, and leaving it at Johnson's Hillock locks beyond Chorley. In time this became part of the L & L. Meanwhile the tunnel at Foulridge had been troublesome, and a great ¾-mile embankment above Burnley took time. But at long last, in 1816, the whole line was complete. The Leigh branch to join the Bridgewater opened in 1820, so the long saga was over.

It had been a tale of Yorkshire-Lancashire co-operation and argument, and of several engineers sometimes differing in their advice. But the sturdy results are there now even if the water-supply, at times, has been a problem.

From the Aire at Leeds the canal soon climbs up to show valley views across the Aire, and via massive staircases of two and three locks comes to the great "five-rise" staircase at Bingley. Here the canal rises 60ft up a hillside, with each lock leading straight to the next via cliff-like gates. Obviously all staircases must be operated carefully, since locks can be either flooded or drained.

Bingley five-lock staircase — afar.

Bingley — close up.

All along from Leeds there seem to have been plenty of trees, and moorland backing even to the towns. But beyond Bingley there is much open country. Swing bridge after swing bridge take you past Keighley and towards quiet Kildwick with its long church. Silsden, next, has two boatyards and huge views up to the moors, then the gateway to the dales, Skipton, is in sight.

This is a very pleasant town for a mooring, and it has a short canal arm, the Springs branch. This runs to the foot of Skipton Castle, and limestone used to be loaded down chutes from a quarry until 1946. Stone is still quarried, but not sent by canal.

A few more miles and swing bridges bring the waterway to locks again at Gargrave — another enjoyable town near the Yorkshire National Park area. Many think the canal stretch by Marton the finest of all, before three locks reach the highest level of water. Beyond Barnoldswick is Foulridge tunnel, famous for a swimming cow in 1912, and built partly by cutting and covering over afterwards.

Now the locks start to drop at Barrowford, and many Lancashire towns lie ahead. Between Nelson and Burnley you are high above a valley and indeed the views are always vast, even past factory chimneys. The high embankment at Burnley gives a grandstand sight of town and moor, and there is a scatter of smaller villages before Blackburn's hilly spread. This is perhaps the most hemmed-in length of canal outside Liverpool, but even here there is an airy embankment beyond the six locks.

From Blackburn to Wigan is a surprisingly refreshing trip, with woods and spring flowers and a delightful group of locks at Johnson's Hillock. Chorley is to one side of this ex-Lancaster Canal length, and later you can see for miles above Wigan before the sharp turn to the great flight of locks. Twenty-one of them drop laboriously down, but skirting the town all the same. Then after the 7½-mile Leigh branch comes in across desolate country, two more locks go out past Wigan Pier and to the Douglas valley.

Even the milestones are sturdy.

Grandstand over Wigan.

The land is flatter now, but still with a few locks until the last one at Appley Bridge. Then the canal sets out on its level sweep to Liverpool. There are shops at Parbold and Burscough, with pubs at several bridges, and Southport not far away. There is also the intriguing Rufford branch to the Douglas at Tarleton, past timbered Rufford Old Hall. The main line eventually approaches Liverpool past Maghull and Aintree racecourse, and into solid Liverpudlian surroundings with the usual city junk.

The end is not a beauty spot, but the four locks down to Stanley Dock are worth seeing — and using.

(with branches) 141 miles, 104 locks, 2 tunnels, 3 main and many small aqueducts, over 50 swing bridges. Parts completed 1774 to 1820.

Manchester Ship Canal

This canal is of academic interest to most pleasure-boaters, since there are strict regulations about ambling on to it in holiday mood. Reasonably so, for huge ocean-going vessels need a lot of room. But the canal is quite fascinating, and many waterway enthusiasts take the boat-trips along it that run from Manchester.

It was dug much later than any other canals apart from a few cuts such as the New Junction and a short length at Limehouse. Completed in 1894, its building was a far cry from the navvies, with their picks and shovels, of the earlier canals. Great machines were used, and 70 million bricks laid, with over 16,000 people employed at one time. Part of the course of the existing Mersey & Irwell Navigation was enlarged, but much was entirely new cutting.

Manchester was already linked with the rest of the canal system in different directions, but only for small vessels. Even the Mersey & Irwell Navigation locks were only 68ft by 17ft 6in. The Ship Canal brought vessels of 15,000 tons into the lower part, and 12,500-tonners to Manchester. The whole canal is in fact the "Port of Manchester", and with docks all along it it is one of our biggest ports, carrying over 5,000 ships a year. The largest of the three entrance locks is 600ft by 80ft, and in four other places there are pairs of locks allowing for ships up to 600ft by 60ft.

View of the canal from the Barton swing aqueduct.

There are extensive docks in Manchester, and the canal can be entered from the Bridgewater via Hulme lock and the upper Irwell. Four miles along it passes under the famous Barton swing aqueduct, and of course there are several swing road-bridges on the route as well as high railway and motorway bridges. The Mersey joins the canal near Irlam (while still small) and leaves again later. Near Warrington are complicated junctions with remaining parts of former navigations.

Eventually the canal approaches the Mersey again at Runcorn, and past flourishing Weston Point docks, and the mouth of the Weaver, takes a remarkable course separated from the Mersey merely by an embankment. There is a link with the Shropshire Union at Ellesmere Port, then at Eastham the Mersey is finally entered, six miles from Liverpool.

36 miles, 5 locks, several swing bridges. Completed 1894.

Pocklington Canal

This canal looks to be well out on a limb. It can be reached by boat only via the tidal Yorkshire Ouse and the Yorkshire Derwent, and is in extensive rural surroundings.

Uncomfortable balance beam at Cottingwith lock.

At one time, however, everyone wanted a canal, and Pocklington was considered in 1767 as a possible branch terminus from a Market Weighton Canal to the Humber. This didn't come off, so in 1801 Pocklington was talking of a canal to the Derwent, and thus to the Ouse. This was eventually agreed in 1814, after various alterations had been suggested. The 9½-mile canal opened in 1818.

One interesting point was that it ended at the turnpike road (now A1079). An extension of about a mile to Pocklington itself was argued, but the extra five locks planned were not agreed in the end. So the terminus is a pleasant lonely basin at Canal Head, with the *Wellington Oak* pub across the nearby road.

In such a thinly-populated area the canal was never very busy, taking such things as coal and manure up to Pocklington, and timber and corn away to the connections westward. And so came the railways. By 1847 there was a line to Pocklington, and canal trade was falling. In 1848 the railway took over the canal, and it then merely staggered along. Gradually the upper end silted up, but a barge still managed to enter in 1932. In 1934 the last known pleasure boat came in. But in 1969 restoration started, and is slowly going up from the Derwent.

Now that the Derwent mouth barrage is built, getting to the canal is easier, since only 6½ miles of tidal Ouse from the Selby Canal need be used. Then 11½ Derwent miles bring boats to the shallow arm to Cottingwith entrance lock, restored in 1972. There is a carefully-guarded nature reserve alongside, and some restored swing-bridges as the route goes through reopened Gardham lock.

Melbourne village is near, but there is very little other habitation. Restoration goes on, with deep locks to deal with, through this quiet area. It may be that the final stretch will take some time yet, except for walkers and canoeists, but it would be a pity not to see boats in the basin again.

9½ miles, 9 locks, some swing bridges. Completed 1818.

Ripon Canal

This was one of the shortest canals in the country, and is now a far-flung outpost of British Waterways. The Yorkshire Ouse and the River Ure to Swale Nab are not under BW, but the Board is responsible for the northern Ure to Oxclose lock, and the Ripon Canal from there. In fact this part of the Ure and the Ripon Canal are treated as a single navigation, with two deep locks along the Ure itself at Milby and Westwick.

The navigation has had a difficult history, first with shoals or low water in the Ure causing trouble with laden boats, then with railway competition, and eventually with railway ownership and neglect. The Ripon Canal, in fact, was to be abandoned in 1956, but the Ripon Motor Boat Club took over the lower 1 ¼ miles, and British Waterways again look after this section now. The rest, with two derelict locks to Ripon, is unusable but still full of water.

Above Swale Nab the Ure itself is often more like a canal, with sharp bends. Boroughbridge is passed by a cut, and Westwick lock leads on past Newby Hall with its collection of chamber pots, and at last to the shallow entrance to Oxclose lock and the canal. This unusual lock (whose paddles are called "clews") is chained with the same special handcuff device as on the Leeds & Liverpool, and you may have to climb up a ladder to get to the gates.

Northernmost navigable bridge in the linked waterway network.

The canal is tidily lined now with the Boat Club boats, along a tree-shaded towpath. The club barge is by the final bridge — the northernmost canal bridge in the connected waterway system. From here you can reach a phone box up a lane, or walk an extremely pleasant towpath to Ripon. This passes the two wrecked locks and a flattened bridge, but skirts canal water all the way to the old basin and the *Navigation Inn*, almost at the foot of the squat cathedral.

1 ¼ miles, 1 lock. Completed 1773.

Rochdale Canal

An intriguing canal, this one, for although as a trans-Pennine route it is supposedly gone, an odd 1 ¼-mile, 9-lock length remains precariously navigable in the heart of Manchester. Moreover, there are lively moves to restore the other 32 miles and 83 locks which took it to the Calder & Hebble at Sowerby Bridge. The part in Manchester is a vital link in the "Cheshire Ring" canals, joining the restored Ashton and Peak Forest Canals with the Bridgewater.

The original canal, like many, had several false starts and arguments with rivals before finally getting under way. It was spurred on by the beginnings of the Leeds & Liverpool, worried by a mooted canal from Bury, and rivalled then by the Huddersfield Narrow Canal. There were surveys by Brindley and Rennie, and eventually William Jessop supervised the building. Rochdale was linked with Sowerby Bridge by 1798, and at last with Manchester, with blue ribbons in everyone's hats, in 1804.

A 3,000yd tunnel was avoided by an extra 14 locks, so that the Rochdale became the heaviest-locked broad canal in the country. It eventually had eight reservoirs to feed it. It passed near Oldham, Rochdale, Todmorden and Hebden Bridge on its way to Sowerby Bridge, from where several Yorkshire towns could be reached.

As a through route it ceased trading by 1937, and most of it was officially closed in 1952. An interesting fact is that it remains in private hands. The Rochdale Canal Co. has many other interests now, and the remaining canal link is something of an embarrassment. The licence fee charged seems high, yet cannot cover the cost of upkeep.

Final shallow length to the Bridgewater.

The short trip now is fascinating. From the Canal Co.'s offices the first lock drops under a tower block near Piccadilly station, and in fact the second lock is in darkness under the block. The remaining shaky locks are often between canyons of other tall buildings, with little sight of the outside world. Water may be cascading over the top gates, but the lower pounds can be very shallow. The final lock enters the debris-strewn Bridgewater, with its 28 level miles to Runcorn.

1 ¼ miles, 9 locks, 1 tunnel. Original canal completed 1804.

Selby Canal (with part of R. Aire)

At one time commercial traffic from Leeds followed the River Aire down to the Yorkshire Ouse. The lowest lock was at Haddlesey, with swift tides below it. This lower stretch often delayed boats, and there were various plans to avoid this, including one for a brand-new canal from Leeds to the Ouse.

In the end a scheme emerged to link the Aire with the Ouse at Selby, by digging a canal from the river above Haddlesey lock. This, in 1778, became the main route for goods, until the great new Knottingley to Goole Canal took trade to the new port of Goole from 1826. Nowadays the Knottingley-Haddlesey-Selby route helps pleasure boats to avoid the worst tides of the Trent and Ouse.

The waterway is in two contrasting parts. A smelly and dirty lock by a tar distillery leads into the winding Aire first, below high sloping banks and with distant power stations seeming to leap about as you twist and turn. The Beal lock is a pleasant halt by a small village with two pubs and a high wooden bridge. More twists eventually run by a few unexpected weeping willows to the flood lock on the left into the artificial canal.

Yorkshire Ouse outside Selby lock.   *Beal lock on the Aire.*

This part is quite different — straight for long stretches, with occasional bridges and a very broad towpath. Primroses are on the banks in spring, and blackberries in autumn. Ahead the tall flour mills and Selby Abbey appear, while the Flying Scotsman may pass over you.

There is a youth hostel on a barge outside the swing bridge into Selby basin, which must be worked by the lock-keeper. The basin is small and often crowded, for outside the lock the Ouse runs fast, bringing foreign coasters. The town and shops are a fair walk, but the road is alongside some of the wharves, where the unloading of ships so far inland is an intriguing sight.

12 miles, 4 locks, 1 swing bridge. Completed 1778.

Sheffield & South Yorkshire Navigation

Trade, shipbuilding and a flowery lock at Thorne.

This is one of those navigations which are partly river, partly canal. Indeed, it originated as the R. Dun (Don) Navigation, but nowadays, with pure canals at each end and many artificial cuts elsewhere, only about a quai ter is still river. It forms an industrial waterway with great potential from the West Riding to the Humber, but its development to continental standards seems dogged by unimaginative officialdom.

It has known cantankerousness before, whether from the old millowners and ironmasters, rival companies, or even internal argument. The "Company of the Proprietors of the Navigation of the River Dun" was a 1733 amalgamation of the powers of Sheffield and Doncaster for making the river navigable from Tinsley (near Sheffield) to Fishlake Ferry near Thorne. Below was the open river to Goole, including the artificial Dutch River section dug by Vermuiden in 1625.

The river had carried traffic to Doncaster for centuries, but the length up to Tinsley was a problem. It was completed at last in 1751, and from there a road had to be provided to Sheffield, about four miles. This upper section from Aldwarke to Tinsley was chopped and changed a good deal afterwards, including considerable new cuts and five new locks in 1835, and a further alignment in 1864 to suit a railway.

Meanwhile the present canal sections at both ends of the Don had appeared. The Stainforth & Keadby was planned in 1793 to give access direct to the Trent, avoiding the fast tides of the Dutch River and Trent Falls. It was nearly 13 miles long, leaving the Dun Navigation by Stainforth lock which led back to the river.

The Sheffield Canal, talked about for some time, had the problem of a steep rise and difficult water-supply. But it was dug by 1819, with 12 locks close together at the Tinsley end. Even today water has to be pumped up from the river below.

The two canals were separate companies, but both were taken into the Dun concern in 1849, and amalgamated with railways in 1850. Then in 1889 a new company, the Sheffield & South Yorkshire Navigation Co., was set up with the idea of taking over the whole waterway and developing it ambitiously. We are still waiting for the latter to happen.

There have been improvements, of course, including the digging of the "New Junction" — a jointly owned link with the Aire & Calder — but the ambitious plans of the original S&SY Co. fell short, though there is still trade to Doncaster and Rotherham today. New container-vessel traffic recently started was stopped by the action of Hull dockers.

Entering the navigation from the tidal Trent at Keadby can be tricky, but above the lock the canal runs wide and deep. It passes several swing bridges and Thorne shipbuilding yards, and probably trains of "Tom Pudding" coal-containers nearer to Doncaster, heading for the New Junction towards Goole.

Doncaster lock is under gloomy bridges, but there is pleasant scenery past Sprotbrough. Even a colliery opposite Conisbrough castle makes little impact, but Mexborough is more obtrusive, though almost impossible of access. At Swinton is the remaining short length of the Dearne & Dove Canal which used to connect with Wakefield. There are still four locks and a well-known boatbuilder.

Beyond Kilnhurst colliery you enter the Don for some distance, leaving again to approach Rotherham through industry. The depot here is the limit of commercial trade at the moment. Rotherham lock is at an awkward angle, with another short river stretch before a cut through the last three locks of the Dun Navigation. Past the top of a weir the canal climb to Sheffield begins.

Under the M1 to the last lap to Sheffield.

The M1 and another lower road bridge tower over the first locks, and a deep lock under railways replaced two earlier ones, making only eleven on the Sheffield Canal now. The others — including one bombed and repaired during the war — soon follow, and the last length is level, with wide industrial views towards moors at first, and multi-coloured water. You are enclosed towards the end, reaching Sheffield Basin after a sharp turn. You can moor near a busy road with good shops and a market opposite.

43 miles, 28 locks, 1 lift and 12 swing bridges. Complete route open 1819.

Odds and Ends

As I mentioned in the introduction to this book, it's not always easy to place waterways in categories. Just as some of the broad canals have locks shorter than normal — and some even have narrow locks in places — so also there are broad-locked lengths on narrow canals.

The present-day Shropshire Union is an interesting example of this, but one easily explained. After travelling northwards for nearly 45 miles through 29 narrow locks, you suddenly meet a staircase pair of broad locks at Bunbury, and the remaining 17 locks on the canal are broad. The broad locks are in fact on the old Chester Canal, built as a barge canal 36 years before the narrow-locked Birmingham & Liverpool Junction came up to meet it at Nantwich.

Chester — Northgate staircase.

Stenson — Trent & Mersey.

A similar reason led to the western Trent & Mersey having a single broad lock at Middlewich, to allow wider boats to come from the Bridgewater — though they had problems with the tunnels (and nowadays couldn't pass narrowed Croxton aqueduct anyhow). Thereafter Trent & Mersey locks are narrow all the way to Burton-on-Trent. But from Burton to the river at Shardlow there are again six broad locks in 16 miles. Thus barges could reach Burton from the Trent. These eastern Trent & Mersey locks are mostly tough ones, too, deep and hard to work, with formidable sills.

The Chesterfield Canal, also, has six broad locks on the 15 miles up to Retford, with all narrow locks beyond. Narrow points in the canal itself prevent use by barges now, however, even if they could tackle the shallow channel.